# Bird on the Horizon

Fluctisonant Press

# Bird on the Horizon

John Henry Rolston

Fluctisonant Press

Copyright © 2016 John Henry Rolston
ISBN 978-1-365-12428-0
First Edition
Cover painting: "Iris (Standing)" Detail
by Michael Fuchs


All Rights Reserved

"Akhenaten
And the great Queen whom he loves, the
Lady of the Two Lands
Nefer-nefru-Aten Nefertiti, living forever."
    - Hymn to the Aten

# **Poems**

| | |
|---|---|
| Inquiline, my poem, | 9 |
| Let me reach across the stars | 11 |
| And You | 12 |
| Not wearily whence the mermaid wanders | 13 |
| I see flowers as I sleep | 14 |
| A willow wiles beside its stream | 15 |
| Such dread this moon who draves the sea | 16 |
| I wish I could live | 17 |
| No sudden songs, no swift scream | 18 |
| Lightning strikes the southern bar | 19 |
| Each night seems the same | 21 |
| It is like holding a wafer at the altar rail | 22 |
| My friend Mudung lives far away | 23 |
| Rocks must have hearts of flowers | 24 |
| How many times have I passed you | 25 |
| Swoosh, sparrow, swoosh | 26 |
| It is my heart you see | 27 |
| Often, but a little | 28 |
| There is not love which can't be bettered | 29 |
| The yellow moon moves with the | 30 |
| Your lavender heart | 31 |
| Fairies sleep when the day explodes | 32 |
| She knit me a cloud | 34 |
| In the smiling sun | 35 |
| What would happen when the wind | 36 |
| I curse the heavens | 37 |
| Hell does not have to hurry | 38 |
| Still, though winds howl harsh | 39 |
| This star stultifies me | 40 |
| My heart lies still | 41 |
| The wind purrs | 42 |
| Dreaming of night | 43 |
| Within the resounds of a cataract | 44 |
| I feel like twelve | 45 |
| With an audience of angels our lips | 46 |
| One time, I remember | 47 |
| Beneath the swan moon | 48 |
| A whale lumbers from pole to pole | 49 |

| | |
|---|---|
| Mysterious, yes, but, | 50 |
| I know I am but | 51 |
| I can bless the butterfly | 52 |
| I leave | 53 |
| Do chomp on the better of | 54 |
| My quiet soul roars with ocean voices | 55 |
| What is when there is | 56 |
| While I stand in the morning trickle | 58 |
| What is this Trinity | 59 |
| Dew in a green leaf | 60 |
| I am a marked monk | 61 |
| Twelve auriculas | 62 |
| Fingers flee to flesh | 63 |
| The mermaid moon is night's miracle | 64 |
| Where the sweet birds sing | 65 |
| I prefer to kneel upon | 66 |
| Found, shivering, pule | 67 |
| That, over there, and there, | 68 |
| I cannot mourn mysteries | 69 |
| With Ethiopia on the horizon | 70 |
| Such a dark beer, on | 71 |
| I see rainbows on sunny days | 72 |
| In the valley I | 73 |
| Be my muse, amor | 74 |
| Would | 76 |
| Will she wear a dress | 77 |
| Said the ogre to the rose | 78 |
| Pieces of the ocean | 79 |
| A river runs forever | 80 |
| I toil not for fruit | 81 |
| The splash of memory, laughing sorrow | 82 |
| In my quarkiness | 83 |
| Our too brief perigee of my ever wandering | 84 |
| I am grabbed by the arms of night | 85 |
| Finally | 87 |
| One day in the spring on the coast of France | 88 |

Inquiline, my poem,

    Nestled among these poems
        These love-flowers
        These motley eggs
    Like hills of holy homage
        Fertile for songs
Praises you
  My own dear nest
  Worn with warbling

Let me reach across the stars
And hold your hand

As the ocean lays its waves
Upon the sand
Let me lap against your breast
- Show me how much magic
       Science is

## And You

Such is me, a walrus, a cactus,
A still pools dragonfly,
But when you whisper
You knit me a cloud
        And necklace me with equations
I become a transversal across emotions
        Cycloidal desires and restraints
I am not in time bounded by a polynomial
I am in a world where x to the zero power is true
        Even when the variable is also zero
I am like light, both particle and wave
--and completely comprehensible
And you....
        You are a Renaissance Lady I see Impressionistically,
An Ansel Adams by Man Ray, a Christian Buddhist,
A Tolstoy Haiku.
But when separated from you by more than a whisper,
I am the ant pacing the tree, the drone
Driven by the degree, a still pools dragon fly
        Dreaming of dreams

Not wearily whence the mermaid wanders
Nor westward toward the winter
Nor eastward towards the was that be
Just here and here with the soothing sea
And the breeze of what cannot breeze

The lying laughter of life has fled
To trick the blinder blinds
And all that remains is the mythical mermaid
Who has other dreams than mine
And the breeze of what cannot breeze

If there could be a be where
Seahorse persiflage in prayers redeemed
And in his jaunt transport his dream
But all that remains is mermaid mystery
And the breeze of what cannot breeze

I know the sun desires the moon
And blesses the night where in it shines
I know the flower blooms its beautiful bloom
Excited for the bee's delight
And the bee for the bumbling bears yearn

Go south to go north
For yesterday toward tomorrow, and
Remember a plinth outshines the statue and
The seahorse is excited for the mermaids' merry excitements
      And at least
The breeze breezes for the breeze
           If not for me

I see flowers as I sleep
And feel them snuggle to my cheek

I see constellations during day
And point out their sensual display

I see atoms as they rotate
And passing muons, and sometimes
Photons splash in colors
As they land upon your face

I see butterflies at night
As they float like feathers to the lazy creek

I see free and I see faithful
Like flowers flown to sleep

A willow wiles beside its stream
Unnerved by the commotion of crows
Brown willow by the blue stream
With red berries growing beside green

The wren is careless of the snake's advance
While it sneaks about the clouds
But the willow watches its winging ways
And smiles that it is so gay

Rain cannot despair the forest floor
Which languor's beneath the leaves
Lovingly remembering the willows' ways
Taught by some wandering deer

Even the tortoise in the driest land
Repeats some vestige of the willows prayer
But the willow sighs a humble breath
- Its silence forever intact

So sleep by the willow if you wish for dreams
Of measuring and calculating roses
And wake with found wisdom and profound rhyme
While the willow wiles beside silence, despite time

Such dread this moon who draves the sea
Despite the flowers desperate need
Of the summer solstice and its sun;

The longing days he'll wait without
The warming face embrace, the lonely
Slough pace of his ceremonial march.

Winter has the priestess hold him gently high
With her amaranthine eye, but summer has him on the altar
Broken and drowned in wine.

How he loves the autumn come with clouds
Close to touch while mountain tops
Wipe their glacier tears as mirthful snow returns.

But this is the time for solemnity as devitalization nears;
This is the time for monkish prayer
And what is to be feared is feared

I wish I could live
        My life over again
I'd live it in a bar
        And curse the books
I'd live it drinking
        And despairing the sun
Joyed by nothing
        But a crepitating stool

A clochard who measures
        A person's wealth
        By the drinks passed to me
My math the volume
        Of beer in any given head
Eristic in nothing but
        Small beer
And definitely not love

No sudden songs, no swift scream
No powerful wind full of winsome rain
No dust, sticks, foam or flecks of trees
Moans, whines, howls or threatening bangs
Pounding surf, itching panes
No gale thrashing the trees above
No thunder rising from the ground below
No wretched ghosts neither gnashing nor prancing
No haunted dreams or dayless days
Stains, stings, painful strains of disbelief
Trickling blood upon stones or
Tracks of mud across the porch
No bursting hearts of woeful mourning
No suffering tears through woeful night
No fears, horrors, no worsening silence
Disasters flooding midnights
Low hiss of snakes or owls eyes floating
No flash of flames, no flare of dreams
No smothering gale full of pummeling ice
Just the slow frightful wait for
Your hand to reach for mine

Lightning strikes the southern bar
Such is the outline of her form
Crawling caterpillars feeding on delicious leaves
Are the seams of her curious dreams
Trees sway to dance her thoughts
Butterflies describe her eyes
Her fingers glow of eternity
And angels trace her angles
While God has caused the breeze to blow
Solely to share her scent:
To be touched by that which touches her
Is all one needs of heaven
Daisies rise among the runes
To display the mystery of her destined origin
Red berries among the purple path
Cry of the fertility of her laugh
Her gypsy legs surround my reality
And like vines twist and bloom
Naked with her river I swim upstream
And beneath the midnight moon muffle screams
A universe of stars reside within each eye
Oceans of joyful sorrow are her sighs
Her breasts are lanterns of holiness
Towers of halos topped by ladybug beacons
Bouquets of flowers make up her thoughts
The sun is warmed by her glow
Those same feet were kissed by Jesus
Those same lips adored by Buddha
Angels, with wings of light, stand by her side
To whom she whispers wisdom and are guided
By her design through the corporeal world
Her thoughts are clouds of puffy light
Vibrant with desires and nourishment
Grass is grown solely for her pleasure
Flowers bloom in hope of her perusal
Love nests within her hair
From which chirping songs of joy draw near
Birds sing her name, bats whirl in carnival
In joy her prayers, squirrels collect her breath

Her feet speak tales of wonder, her toes
Contain wisdom unspeakable, her dark eyes inspire
My verse like so many flawed flowers bestowed
Blooms and fades simply to praise the passing of her days
Unworshipped and unknown, the angels blare her name
So all may hear, too late, a saint walked their lake
Giving hope and love to all and someone to emulate

Each night seems the same
        A jerrican of fresh tears
Each day sees the same

Shady people ped
        Outrageously pretentious
dling bright colors

A circling finger
        To semaphore a quick need
For another scotch

"Care for a tot, ma'am?"
        "Fancy a gallop, monsieur?"
The old gargoyle

Your breast beside me
        Tapenade and estouffade
Pinot Grigio

I love the songs which
        The stones beneath boulders sing
From below the brook

I love the poems which
        The young Hieronymus Bosch
Would recite if not for fear

Not so much the path
        Which refused me passage
----But I understand

Soporific thoughts
        Dreams of your breasts beside me
And the rain outside

"What? Vespers again?"
        And with tonsure beneath cowl,
Discalced I bow

It is like holding a wafer at the altar rail
Cupped gently in my palms – she is too precious to taste
It is like watching a lotus flower float beneath
My red bridge – my gaze does not disturb her kindness

Her heart is full of morning dew each holding within
Silent rainbows, each a caterpillars or robins potion
The tall grass giggles with her gleefulness
While the crickets whisper of her wonderful wanton dress

The mountain hermit breathes her name, the violin
Softly describes her face, the ocean breeze – sacred
Wanderer of space – slopes quickly to secretly
Caress her lips in its dreams then slowly flow back to sea…

A bowl of petals on the bench, a grassy cloud for
Angels rest, a quiet dark rich with elegance
- And I, I praying thankfulness with all the rest
For this space upon the arched red bridge

My friend Mudung lives far away
But sometimes I feel a mist
    Upon my face
That I swear had recently
    Been upon hers

Sometimes, a tiger butterfly will
Quietly flit by with
    Such a scent
Unmistakenly of Mudungs moss
That I must quietly rest
    In remembrance

So distant-close to me
It seems my kiss certainly falls
    Upon her lips
And softly fingers move the hair
    To behind her gentle
    Fragrant ear

Rocks must have hearts of flowers
For why else would the winter bees
Be resting upon their backs

Waves must be their dreams then
Thrust out from the hopes
To which they cling

Their souls need be the herons
Which stare and stand for hours
Gathering the quiet within their beaks
To carry for company on their long flights

Indeed, the butterflies must be
The very rocks upon which I've sometimes trod

How many times have I passed you
House by the railroad
Asleep and awake
On my way to my return
How many times have I seen you
As I stood cautiously
Within the door
On my way to my return
How many trains have passed you here
How many lives caught
And lost a glimpse
On their way or their return
How can the many not know your grace
I can fully understand
As the beauty of the rails the many also
Fail to fully feel
So how many times shall I pass you
With your curtain long and the shadow drawn
And fail to pause upon your porch
House by the railroad

Swoosh, sparrow, swoosh
Or nestle quietly in your nest
(Your brood of thoughts restlessly
Pecking at their shelled life)
        Linger at your bath
        Or dawdle over dinner
        I shall sit upon my perch
        And enjoy your behavior

It is my heart you see
        Floating on the sea
My love is a lonely vessel
        Adrift within your heart
"Ahoy" I cry and ahoy
        I sing, but for the echo it brings

It's my heart you see
        Floating on the sea
Encased within your gentle heart
        A safe haven may I never leave
A bay, may it never drain

        A dead sailor nestles in the nest
A ghost whirls the wheel with ease
        And I, with the glass upon my eye,
Beware the ground and despair the sea

My love is an anchored vessel, hear,
        Harpooned upon your heart
Ahoy I sing for the ahoy it brings
        Lest I be lost at sea

Often, but a little
At a time,
Like poor old Swann

There is no love which can't be bettered
Suffering and hope
    Living the sky's caprices
Irrationally
It does not avail
    To avert accusation
Suspiration
Vacant and roomy
    As an untenanted house
My senescence love
Such an abbey ant
Puerile in expression
Inexorable
    Comets piercing skies
Moons lips caressing the suns
    Surreality
    Scurrility
Surreptitiously
With ferruginous hazard
    Your smile enlightens
Your orris root breath
Your wild currant bush desires
--- Places of refuge
Kaleidoscopic
    Simple smile of the sun
Transubstantiate
My recusant heart
Follows her still
    Steadfastly
Invisible sun
There is no hope that can't be bettered

The yellow moon moves with the
        Movement of my soul:
Unchanging, always near, enchanting;
        Predictable, yet confined

Nocturnal joys of bats and owls
        Their screech
Which gives life in the empty night,
        And the hush which comes after,
Their breathing which gives rhythm
        To my thoughts
Sometimes startles my untamed heart.

I circle the night lit streets of the city
Like planets circle the heavens, going nowhere;
And my emotions circle me like so many moons
With the taste of your body on their virgin tongues.

        My embattled lust shackled to the mast
        Tortured by desire and unfulfillment
        Imagine a wave always withdrawing
        Never cresting never rushing
                Never falling
        And the island shall soon slip past

I walk between Scylla and Charybdis
My thoughts wander to Saturn and Venus
Your eyes and your smile bid me welcome...
        Toward the rockbound coast
        I am drawn
        But – before the risk of adventure
                I drown

Your lavender heart
        Stands but among the flowers
Like the orange sun

Secret messages
        Enclosed in tiny bottles
Enclosed in my heart

Hot winter mornings
        And the coolness of your thoughts
Give my heart balance

Your quiet breathing
        Reminds me of the heavens
White clouds drifting by

Rocky river beds
        Rust-red speckles flashing by
And your reflection

Like a butterfly
        Alive in a green casket
--or was it yellow?

Lucky, the strangers
        Benefitting from fall rain.
Growth comes from skies' tears

Fairies sleep when the day explodes
In leafy abodes in dancing dreams
By distant streams they live uncaught
Cloudy thoughts give clear visions
Sometimes prisons but always heaven
Different brethren are different met
Expressing the best of inner conceit

Planets pound their paths with constant ease
Careless terrified granite in a constant affair
With darkness, fairness and the cold relief of space
Comets come in bliss concrete exploring
Haste desiring a nest but flailing past
Tender and in grace   Would that heaven had no
Chair in which to render from their expelled air

When I sleep the night implodes
My thoughtful groves and I live by love
And lips above and below my closed stare
With coarse care and gentle smiles
The sensual style of your fairy legs
My heart enslaves to awaken among
A lullaby sung by sheep

Time treks and takes its pauses refreshing
Beneath the pines sipping upon dew
Storytelling with a wreath of poppies
Funny sad silly sorrowful and terrible
Wrens upon sundry limbs sulk and sing
As the past pretends to disappear and the
Fake present dances as if near

We twirl sleepless in sleep, dreamful in
Dreams within dreams, asleep to them
Night which befalls us giving
Lightless light to the country side and
With butterfly eyes espying the aura of
Love it is not light our desire but seeming light
Which light gives painful death its smile

Stars exposed mount unseen in distant spaces
Engrossed lonely afar beauty perfectly displaced in
Unending epitaxy posted across galaxies
With a grapey shimmer bending a simple grandiosity
Like a Madonna lily writhed through the sky as
A guided kite without purpose sinuous:
Out of Sheol its guised senseless Shelta synthesizes my life

Your sleep is wakefulness esteemed by fairies
Sitting upon berries transfixed in ecstasy erotic
Estuary of symbolic turtle thoughts night has no policy
For understanding the embassy of your bare body
Electric tenderness embroidery of the sky is in your eyes
And across your cries fairy energy is memory alive
In your sleep ending in perfect endlessness

She knit me a cloud
A scarf of condensation

The sheepish cloud
Twisting into gentle shapes
Caressing mountain tops
Pillows for the heads of trees
After floating on the warm summer breeze
In winter chills the valley floor
While the solid cresting powerful waves
Crash a thousand days into a thousand tears
While I crave the scent of flowers
But fear the stare of the full moons bloom
I would ride on a white horse to you
To arrive silently drink tea
Your lips are part dream
Memory and wish
Fulminating furtherance

In the smiling sun
In the flowers hidden grace
I can trace your face

Hidden by your hair
The stars are everywhere, like
Flowers in the sky

I can see the moon
Hiding behind falling snow
Beyond the mountain

Lugubrious love
Scent of lovage lurks at night
Nautilus living

In the wind I write
And in the wind you can read
The imprimatur

Good-humoredly
The golden glowworm delights
In my deliquesce

What would happen when the wind
Stops wandering and the leaves are
        Left in peace
Wondrous skies may begin to fill
With more wondrous fears and cloud
        The leaves from heat
The sacred stillness may not seem so discrete
Burdening the waveless lake with disease
And in the silence leave the night to dream
All the cares it was wantless in the day

What happens when the wind begins to play
And the leaves again tremble in pleasure
        And in pain

I curse the heavens
        The wicked sky
                Wild and feckless
                      On its own
Yet so constrictive
        To me

So wanton
        And demanding me
                Wantonless

Un appointed
        I kneel
                To you
Not
        To be anointed
But that my conventional
                Heart
Might simply contemplate
        Your
                Sacerdotalism

Hell does not have to hurry
Heaven should not have to hasten
Slumbering under a sleeping sun
A troglodytic moon truckles to time

So little has he who loves a lot
And a lot he who so little
The sun shines as bright on a cloudy day

But childhood must slip away
From the shore of an adults play
For winters snow in springs abode
Cannot be much adored

I.
Still, though winds howl harsh
A miracle butterfly
Glows while the day ends

II.
Strange to be so glad
When surrounded by rain
- To smile through mist
- Dance in dreary dew

And odd to be frightened
By a butterfly
Or to wander lost
    Along known paths
And stand gusted by
    Soft breezes

But here it is, the suns
    Midnight prayer
    Through the clouds
And a werewolf purring
    Outside town:
Beautiful waves have
Turbulent ebbs and
    Light shrouds darkness
    While I hum silence

III.
Lugubriously
Like a sandy Laayoune moon
To forfend my heart

IV.
Love, like a great Auk,
Wanders like a dreamed moon
Lighting my dark path

This star stultifies me
Appearing as it has
A seeming blind eye
Staring me into submission
    Of sin
With its silent paroxysms

Like Gods' faithful secretary
A transfixed hound
An ember in the ice fields of Heaven
Gleam in the eye of a
Grateful goat
The illusion of an illusion
Patterned after chaos

Such a striking star
Corresponding to a star in my heart
Weakening my wealth of happiness
Staring me into supervention
    Of sin
With its wanton watchfulness

My heart lies still
With a hibernating soul;
Winter seems less cold

You must forgive me
(pale moon transgressing blue sky)
My unworthiness

Symmetry breaking
: Distinct in the universe
Obstreperousness

In lazy blossoms
My dream relax splendidly
Beneath mornings fog

Two leaves in one pond
Float on a reflected moon;
A willow smiling

Our lips kiss:
A particle created;
All things from nothing

Window reflection…
It is nice to have your eyes
So close to my poem

        The wind purrs  
As my hand gently kisses  
        The lovely petals  
Of its ghostly back

And the sea so thoughtfully  
        Sings  
Like a grey mouse from its  
           Grey field  
Through the fog  
                From its memory

I remember more than I have  
        Experienced  
Things so dear, petals plucked  
        And pushed into my graveyard pockets  
To wait for another look  
        At a wind-soaked welcome

    Dreaming of night
Changing my life
   Into wine
I dream of night
    Of foggy umbrellas
And touchless canvases
    With floating paint
$\frac{x}{0}$ and $\sqrt{-1}$
    In other words
My life
    But all life has a
Source of light
    As even deaf ears
Have music

I hold you close, defining
The red shift of your spectrum
I track your presence, despite
The imaginariness of your number

Picasso dreams
    Chagall realities
Like an umbrella
    On a foggy day

Within the resounds of a cataract
        All sound of earth are unbrung
The swift steel thread through the
        Devils' jungle
In blankets float in an angels fall
Timeless like golden light in slow slow motion
Drip from the sky forever
        Around me
And with my sight obscuring
        Towards colorful blindness
The hush of the roar becomes prayer
And the quiet of the thunder
        Turns outside blurry

I feel like twelve
        Divided by thirty-seven
        Less than half a man

And forty-seven fingers on
        Three quarters of a dozen hands
        Is not enough to count

Put an obol under my tongue
        For I am ready
I have a noon-time shadow
- In June
- Near the Tropic of Cancer

I ask for nothing more
Than to lay beneath a cooling breeze
Upon a lawn of blues and greens
And be a witness to the intimate life
Of beautiful, passing clouds
As passing geese would quickly lose their way
If not for the stunning scenery, which makes
        Them grateful slaves
As vibrant rivers suddenly turn to graves
If their race through gorge from lake is taken away
As I if from this dream be carelessly awakened

With an audience of angels our lips
Meet like hands in prayer, mumbling
Magic messages of childish desires:
Little leaves which haven't much
Leverage left, waving in the gentle
Wind, ready to slip from limb to trunk;
Like doorways to chancel, your lips draped
In chasuble, cloaked in wisdom and
Scented with mystery; your heptamerous
Kisses on my Herculaneum lips; our
Hephaestus love, our lips, our kiss…
Basking beneath the blue eyes of God
Our lips separate like hands in praise, speaking
Spells stolen from the books of heaven:
Vesperal words protecting the secrets
Vibrating in clouds, chosen to describe
Your beauty and blessedness, choices
Given to us: your memnon heart, immortal
Now, whose music greets my melpomene
Mornings, our menarche love, my menhir
Heart, our lips, our kiss….

One time, I remember,
        Not long ago, other
Snowmen stood, now gone
        Now mere ghosts of joy
But I remember, as I shall
        These others,
After all have forgotten all the snowmen
        In their lives
Snowmen skillfully sewn together
        By childish hands
Chiseled in the cold and
        Honored for some qualities
Both magical and religious:
        Stand cold, melting in
The movement of this
        Changing season
Slowly, no longer tall,
        Shaped only a hint
Of their former selves

Beneath the swan moon
Your dreams drift with gentle thoughts
Which ripple my creeds

About or afar –
You are my flowers feather
Floating with the breeze

The moon rises and,
       Like a halo, surrounds you
Beautifully

Lovely like a lake
Still green with a blue quiet
Rippling the shore

Roses recherché
A vespertine valentine
Polypetalous

She flies through the sky
With visions of Atlantis
She closes her eyes
Then closes her eyes
Her head leans on mine

The clouded moon hides
Our promiscuousness
As shy as shyness

A whale lumbers from pole to pole
    Like a tenement dweller wanders the halls
As a sea snail from continent to continent crawls
    Writing poems along unseen ocean floors
An unnoted leaf tumbles along the busy street
    Like a sleepy vagrant pushed from door to door
While all the while a white rose
    Whittles it witness in Borromean rings

Mysterious, yes, but,
The sea has not secrets;
The bumblebee sometimes
Has a lazy day
When with butterfly thoughts
It dreams of forest flowers.

The sea does not hide its treasures,
Though difficult to discover
And I once watched an ant
Stand and stare for hours
Upon a country side
Before it continued upon its path

I know I am but
One trinket about your wrist
But I bless this bed

Neck, back, belly, ribs
My kisses drizzle her head
        Dream aureola

Birds walking on stilts
Fish carrying umbrellas
Worms using shovels

It must be the worms
        Causing birds to smile so
And the fish to sing

Bee buzzing about
Draves to drown in my dark blood
My vespertine heart

I lay by the lake
        Under a cheerleader moon
And dream about math

A quiet turtle
- Suddenly its head retreats
I put on more tea

You must forgive me
Pale moon transgressing blue sky
My unworthiness

While clouds cover stars
Waves recede and moons descend
        - All the sand remains

Life is filled with secrets
You can't learn them all at once, or young

I can bless the butterfly
With my hand upon the limb
While the trail moves on far below me
And the wind wanders within my mouth

I can give sanctuary to the flower
Growing wild upon this mountain
And protect all the ruling rocks
From dust ruining rebel raindrops

And like Peter I'll open wide
Allowing the forgiven sky
As Charon I will lead the river
Like a caterpillar along my finger

But my eyes wander steady
On a leaf in circular retreat
A brown orb against the white
        Forest floor
With a seed within its palm

I leave
Shoulder length to the moon
Cascading with the seeming stars
To the waiting ocean
      Of earth

I was with Olympians
Conversing with the very
      Goddess
Of heath heavenly bodies hearing
Nearby music magic me
      To Eden

Want I always now the then
The angels' length of hair
Touching always my face
This ocean of earth always below her lace

Do chomp on the better of
The large glass
Tasty but tart telling
Much more than it tells.  Even
Can a green box hold the
      Secrets of my heart
Slips of Fortunes inside my
      Veins cancelled forever.  Faint
She is eternally mine/not mine
And though I shout she
Can't hear silence, but
At least we shared a bench
Once
Like Gabrielle in Jura with
      Me, DuChamp

My quiet soul roars with ocean voices
Hushed by naiads and seahorses
So only those upon the sand can listen
Though not understand the enlisted

Jungle emotions appear as pastures
Which lambs and geese stroll uncaptured
But it is the caged beasts which are most free
Which is witnessed by my heart at peace

When sultans become the most Christian
We shall know the truth has risen
And when Christians finally abide by Buddha
Jesus will have found fruition

Still the storm rages unnoticed
Except by the cold brush of the artist
Who even then with a sly pen
Titles the torture "The Calm Ocean"

What is when there is//colors when there is no sight
        Sounds which make no noise
Delta has sigma//there is fire in the ice
        Quanta are cosmic
Snow falls in deserts//stars linger during day
        I am near, afar
Isn't it the same//as the growing of the grass
        Or the falling leaf
The jussive beating//of the blue butterflies wings
        And my orange heart
My simple life is//sacred like a dung beetle
        --pattern not purpose
Witness the wild wave//crushed rock becomes soft sand
        Between your pink toes
There is no mistake//the flower must be taken
        When gently given
And when day is done//that is the time for penance
        And not the moment
Shouldn't we praise the rain//and give the thunder its due
        Thorns are lovely too
Thus is loveliness//borne from her blind loneliness
        Combed through my hair
While breastly visions//float like hieroglyphic clouds
        Through each constant breath
And my empty hands//are testaments of failure
        And my wickedness
And yet I dream on//and still the butterfly flies
        While the worm wiggles
Autumn thoughts of spring//summer sand and winter sea
        A brown nest for soup
But where do bears sleep//when the caves are full of dreams
        And the snow descends
Where does the bee sleep//conspiring desire
        Afar and farther
Yellow scented dusk//ascends in solemn ascent
        And still I pretend
Can duck with the swan//can hell with the heavenly
        Before the dusk dawns
Can rain kiss the sky//does cloud wed the mountain

        Outside imagine
I drive to attack//like a pitiable king
        Towards all but mate
Buddha sleeps and dreams//chaos so predictable
        Orange and creamy
With a little black//the spent bee sleeps with the bear
        And I with the fair

While I stand in the morning trickle
In the center of this estate
I watch the puff of
Gentle flowers like sparkles on dew
Flash individually before me momentarily
--only one is most beautiful and I linger
      Long to listen and smell; off
In the distance the imperceptible sound
Of a train adds credence to my tears

I now know how Mr. Gam Jue stood, so
Silently still; living somewhere else
Than where he stood: alive again in
Some Chinese park, abreast with his lover
And tangled with bliss. So sad a sight we
See, not knowing the gladness of his being.

Is it true: this is the key to a secret
World that only kissing lips can reveal

What is this Trinity
        You and I
Which I sense
        How do we touch
Across some unknown gulf
Like several rainbows
        Intersecting hope

How is it
        Prism hearts
Holy initiation into
        Mystery
Wobble-like like planets
With three poles confusing
        Equators

Dew in a green leaf
Reflecting a troubled moon;
A lady bugs lake

My touch lays bottled
Like a garden on your desk;
Only painted dreams

Like an unkissed butterfly
Stung by your beauty
The honey graces the pain

Stars are like my heart
Marvelous and mythical
A garden of night

Mirroring the galaxies
Blessing your contours
Ablaze with desire

Stars, quiet and shy,
Distant, glum and barely bright,
Destined to drave day

Yellow butterfly
With dangerous desire
Strays from the flower

I am a marked monk
Marred by the mold of dust
Always with one eye only
On the soul
Banished from one world
Self-exiled from the other
Both feet in the stream, but
Both hands on the fruit
Transvestion of thoughts
Who hungers, though sated
Who shivers, though warm
I dream of myself sleeping
Who palms aloe on the stigmata

Twelve auriculas
Hallow your hallowed head
Velvet and primrose

Like me, the blue wind
Whistling in the wild wood
Smiles triumphantly

Golden bees gather
With a Bolshevistic hum
So like white angels

Your spirit, alive,
Like a sea-anemone,
Heaven and haven

Like my lonely love
My poems are turtles. Like me,
Kierkegaardian

Sorrow begets joy;
Would that I were always sad
To spare the sorrow

Halo of the moon
In the path like Balaam's ass
    Keeps me from my dreams

Fingers flee to flesh
As winding worlds sail hearts sea
And her lips port dream

Anisotropic
Tintinnabulation
Of my church bell heart

My heart does witness
Soft soul of simplicity
Your invariance

Blessed butterfly
Flickering beautiful flight
Toward the unknown

Like a brown tree owl
Or a robed desert monk
Non baryonic

Hearts have openings
Where blood pours out boiling
Scalding the white rocks

Mi sol y luna
Secret of my secret soul
Shadow growing grass

The mermaid moon is night's miracle
Always answering even unprayed prayers
Not like the lying waves which laughingly
Promise then steal away
Not like the beautiful roses
Which bloom beautifully then fade
Not like the warming sun who
Suddenly blisters then skulks
       Coldly behind cold clouds
Not Matthew 11:28 whose green leaf
Crinkles to Matthew 16:24

But the mermaid moon is constant and
Moves with my moves
Seeking out the shards of souls disarrayed
And pieces together the dreams of the dreamless
       To undead the dead
            Like me

Where the sweet birds sing
As pan whirling sweet syrinx
The serpent hisses

Heliolatries
Antinomianism
Luminosity

As her icy eyes
Melt, cold tears roll off her cheek
To the frozen ground

Kempt, just as sunshine,
Specially in the fog of
Vulgar transcendence

Vagabond planets
Running wild through the vineyards
Ripe with streetlight stars

The butterfly sings
Bringing tears to a raindrop
Suddenly happy

I prefer to kneel upon
    Knobby pews
And know the relic'd marble
    Altars well

Still, I bear the Trappist truth
With Jesuit demeanor

And know bees favor unfaded flowers
And angels care for cherubim curvaceousness
And rivers opt for oceans

Found, shivering, pule
Among the clouds, stars and snow
You naked baby
The Quezada moon,
Beautiful pregnant mother,
Rosy cheeks and all
Obsequiously
The queen will flatter your way
With petals and psalm
Look up to the moon
Her rosy lovely smile
Dodecahedron
Puppy clouds at night
Play like kittens with her mouth
Purring with delight
Hermit songs belong
Far below and farther flung
To be hums of waves
Merely monkish mists
Shrouding rocks and craggy cliffs
Crawling for a peek
Marvel all the woods
Which crave the light of her gleam
So the critters pray
Even in dark deep
With knowing dreams of her glow
Sparkle all the gold
So me, softly close,
Softly treading her shadow,
Softly fear the most
The Quezada moon
Mother of our cherished rose
Smiles and flowers bloom
Butterflies may bring
-O, could I forever dream –
Your lips to my cell

That, over there, and there,
Concerts, had there been music,
Waves, had there been water,
And decorated with copper
If all the ants and bees had had their way

But here, where clouds speak
And wingless angels ride bawdy butterflies
And you and I and others, had wind blown
Some skies should be wrapped in clouds
And decorated with pearls
If any ants dreams had come true

Dwarf trees stand tall like hunch-backed giants
Crying their tears of leaves upon the floor
If only there were more feathers for the birds
Rapt roses wrapped in spider threads
And decorated with berries
Had the bees prayers ever been blessed

Why couldn't the lazy sun dawdle well past dusk
And ants tarry til dawn and rest in bark
Bees by droves invite the moths to dine with wine
Lazy lakes could entertain the oceans lust
And decorated by moonlit kisses
The vine could entwine twin heavens

I cannot mourn mysteries
Unexplained, manifested without definitions
Lines without equations, flowers
Without petals, gentleness
Without gentleness

I cannot question rain without clouds
Nor weep for losses never found,
Circles without radii, fire
Without fuel or flames, love without love

And yet I must listen to voices
That never speak, comprehend and obey
Precisely orders laid unordered
Quantify the uncountable
With count and suffering and love

Decidedly I had decided long before the decision
Broken the bread and gulped the wine:
If I cannot circumspect and quench
Then let my hunger multiply

With Ethiopia on the horizon
      How did I arrive in Egypt
          -Again

She glanced back, and I turned to salt
The sun which glanced upon the earth
Meekly surrendered to clouds

I almost caught the falling leaf
I almost felt a cooling breeze
The word was almost there but the poem escaped
She glanced back, and I, well I,
      Stand like salt and stare

I have yet to say hello and must bid goodbye
My rainbow smile turns to taste the tears

Why am I awakened just as dusk appears

        Such a dark beer, on
Such a little evening
           Shouldn't she be here

        Across the dark room
So many loneliness's
          Flicker in silence

        While they are merely
Revolving constellations;
          I am the Pole Star

        I am though there is,
Lovers swear true beneath me;
          Pirates guide by me

Cyclops of the Argus sky

Still I blaze in vain
            Unseen by southern sailors
And the sleeping sea

I see rainbows on sunny days
    When cloudy thoughts sometimes take shapes
Birds, in trees, sing the tale of my dreams
    While mermaids wander about my room
        Discussing my shoes
Then, green flames of the bonfire of trees
    Race across my memories
The yellow rain of leaves upon my sleep
    Could be butterflies
        Listening to me breathe

And Eros sitting with empty bow, smiling
    And scratching his nose
While the cool evening's breeze gently
    Brushes across my eyes and
        Bids me to awake
In the sunny vale this night
    I make new shapes from the orient stars
It is true – broken rainbows
    Make beautiful gardens

In the valley I
        Stared up at the mountain
And wondered what
        Was hidden by
                The jealous clouds
- The jaded dragons or
Brilliant jewelry on
                Rusted chains
Or maybe just a burdened bear
Timidly scratching his back

One day I walked toward
        The welcoming call
And wound the circular way
                To the mountains top
Cold and sore I finally stopped
Midst a shroud of fog
        And wondered –
What are those lights
And why are they dancing
                Like stars in a
                Forgotten puddle

Be my muse, amor  
(Christ of my doubting Thomas)  
A yellow duck upon the blue water  
Of my thoughts and dreams -  
Cool fresh water upon the craggy  
Rock which is my heart -  
Be the angel which stands beside  
With wings of inspirations -  
    A breath as close as a kiss.  
Be more muse than amor, amor  
A face upon the still green water  
Whose hand I dare not reach  
      A heaven unapproachable,  
       A Goddess with a goddess face  
Be the butterfly with paisley blue  
And sparkling silver wings  
Which brushes against my cheek  
And lands upon the lake-  
Have the breasts whose milk I taste  
So when I wake the dream remains  
That below I may take my midnight strolls  
With the suns glow above.  
Amuse me to be my muse, amor  
No need to beware of more  
Tragic for me but bliss for you  
A cloud for shadow but not for rain  
A butterfly whose random flight  
Has meaning to me  
(Christ of my denying Peter)  
Cool water upon the craggy heart  
Which is my rock.  
Be more amor than muse, amor  
More silent-kisses of a mountain  
Than a watchful rivers image -  
An ocean in orange-ruby bloom  
To amuse the moon -  
A rose cradled and smelt!  
Be the welcoming tree  
    *Ravageable*

So I, the foraying wind,
May run my body through your limbs
And jitter your leaves:
Be more amor than amor, amor
(Christ of my crucified Christ)
(Nothing less) / (nothing more) than what
You already are:
Cool water which melts the rock
Which is my heart

Would
That I could have waiting
Black crow feathers
Strewn before me
        Like palms
As I enter the strange new city
Beyond the broken past
Would
That I could have
Mermaid arms wrapped
About me seaweed tight
        As I float
Towards the moons hovering smoke
Above the horizon

Black swans
Upon the lake
Vinculums between
Her and everything
        Her heaven and me
Would that the panthers breath
Would hold me in sleep
But
The hyena in dream
With ludicrous laughter
Lulls me awake
        While
The crow pecks pestering
The papers flown about the floor

Will she wear a dress
    For me tonight
Will she wear a little less
    Which dares
        My caress
Will I have a chance
    To behold
A flash of flesh
        Beneath
    The concealed revealed
A sudden glimpse, a scent
    Of heavens bliss
A gift of celestial
        Augustness
    Perhaps
Will she taunt me, test me
    Arrest me
Will she allow an ounce
    Of cherishing
        And perishing
Won't she terrorize me
Embarrass me
    Agonize me
While I must merely
    Sit forced
        Respectfully

"The love of beauty is not for the meek of heart" – Art Bridge

Said the ogre to the rose
I feel the full force of my eros
When I behold you, and grow faint with desire
And the wicked beast within me would wrest
Your loveliness from the stalk
And press you to my breast,
        Thorns and all;
But to lay illicit claim to beauty
Is a demonic act
And, though ugly, I am no thief
So please suffer my suffering gaze
And ignore my breathless whispers
As I press my rapacious lips to your imagined breast
        And brave the pain that thorns abhor

Pieces of the ocean
(parts of the whole)
All about [us:snug]
Like Blake's minute
Particles, each as
Important as the other:
(Leibniz opposed and
Confirmed):
But my favorite: the
Raindrop
Living between lips

A river runs forever
  But not forever
The eternal sun
  Must someday
    Lose its day

There is not a rock
  In the universe
Which once
  Did not exist

Morning threats, then
  Evening events
And yet there is the noon
  And more

I toil, not for fruit
Sleep, not for rest
Eat, not to live

A zeugma of society
Aspirating conversation
A desert father of
The beach
A milkweed without
Monarch;
The rutilant rocks
      Like stone lips
Lying beside the river

I crawl, not for measure
But only for the mirage
Of a rufous sun
Above a pinkish sea

## MERMAID SONNET

The splash of memory, laughing sorrow,
Gives air its splash of mist and mind its trail
Traced yesterday and today its morrow.
Tomorrow's certain as the past is frail!:
Swim into the current of the future,
With fairies fluttering along the way,
Resting in contours of the wooded pools.
The splash creates a bountiful parade
Which brings full sudden sad smiles, Neptune grown;
If ever there were fairies on the shore
Of my thoughts, even Oberon, behold:
The silence of the prayer envelops
On every petal of every flower
Ever ador'd whispers of you, flower…..

In my quarkiness
        I am red and green and blue
A bit unglued

Parallel to you
        Perpetually dreaming
Perpendicular

I am drawn to you
        Purely by divine physics:
Gravitational!

Trapezoidal bee;
        Beautiful butterfly;
Hiker by the stream

My reality
        An imaginary kiss
$$\sqrt{-1}$$

If she is matter
        I am her antimatter
Had we kissed – poof

Our too brief perigee of my ever wandering
Pattered out like a stony vagabond
Usual even in this chaos of planets
        Like a dead star blazing in my living sky
        Time is a mystery left like me unrecognized

Don't bring the ocean to my shore
Distracting clouds of swirling brine
Though full lays empty to my eyes
        Its moon a mere motion merely alive
        Its expanse a shimmering shadow asleep

The oscillations of a visceral heart
Roiling the relationship between sea and sky
Wise willow keep your wisdom
        Give me the full emptiness of space
        Where invisible life exists

I am grabbed by the arms of night, dragged through
        The mountains and thrown toward the ocean
Thrown gracelessly like the last prayers yawned out
        Before the church doors are locked
Thrown as the dawn begins to change the sky and save the land
        From fears of the forever-darkness
But I never enter the wave crashing toward me; the wave
        Thrown from the ocean and I never meet

I wake and enter the waiting day with its harsh
        Determined shadows and measured tones
I walk willingly past the waiting bus and off the curb
        To avoid the willows web
Past the waiting beggars and past the passing strangers
        And past the open church doors
And into the park where I rest by the elm
        Apart from the family resting on blankets
            Whose baby stares at me like I don't belong,
            Like a planet who shouldn't be out of the sky

I am levitated by the dark magician, floated through the air and
        Sped into space toward the edge
Sped carelessly without cause and without orbit on a dangerous
        But sure path toward an uncertain end
Sped without I Ching or Rosary past watching planets and
        Causeless suns without care
But I speed without motion, without turning or turbulence:
        The edge always distant, never nearer, never known

I leave the park and enter the traffic with its peering faces
        Into my life and dreams
Huddled close, I cross streets and wild cries and
        Wicked ambulances racing time
I cross illegally to avoid the temples of Jehovah
        And Mohammed and Vishnu
--- Dreamers, all of them, and foretellers of misery

>    And loneliness and separation
>    --- Commanders of sacrifice and sorrow:
>    Planets. Planets who shouldn't be out of the sky

I am entombed by the gullible gravedigger, pounded into
> The hole of life to wiggle through the earth toward the core
Wiggle without sight or a way, just down
> Toward the airless heat, into the rock
Leaving only dust behind, toward the unknown.
> With tears making the way easier, with sobs no
One can hear; leaving behind only a dark cavern and
> Toward the molten core which would be death to reach

I sit quietly at my coffee (beside the train tracks which
> Lead into the desert and across the snowy mountains)
Listening for the rumbling which foretells the trains
> Leaving or returning: the train which is my god.
When I was a child the train destroyed the image of Caesar;
> As an adolescent I rested in its belly from the world
Now the scourged slowly steps the measured lane to Golgotha
> (speaking to its sons and sisters along the way
>> Who stare and are guilty of something unstateable)
> Like a planet who should not be out of the sky

I am breathed into invisibility by the mouth which comes out
> Of the darkness and swallows the train and never closes
I am disappearing without lighting the candle, disappearing
> Without touching the image of worship
Disappearing and leaving behind foreign hands which
> Shall cup the breasts of my virgin mother
And bring the realization of my dreams to a beginning and an end:
> Disappearing but, alas, not leaving

Finally
After so many years topped
Daily by pigeons
The statue is beginning
To crumble
Visually
Lots of chips here and there
Insignificantly
But now it can be seen
Visually to lean
A crevice created and clearly
Ready to tumble
I remember when it was
Finally installed
After years of regret and
Anticipation
Shiny and sparkling with
Glints from the sun
It was spoken of and pointed at
And with pride pronounced to passing visitors
Until it wasn't
Until finally it was forgotten
Even by pigeons that even still flocked
Upon it, ignorant of its presence
Finally it is dissolving
Unknowingly by all but me
Who watches not woefully and records its
Last moments until
Finally we are finally gone

One day in the spring on the coast of France
In Toulon as the gulls fly in from the sea
And the wind blows out off the land,
You will walk
With a song on your lips and a green rose
In your hair
Your blouse buttoned low and your eyes
Directed at the harbor
Or at a stranger or at the color
Of the fallen leaf from some willow tree
- Had I just looked up from poetry,
Had I simply felt
The crossing of your shadow upon me
And accepted fates last
Hand at correcting its blunder
      Our mystery would be calmed
And my gentle gentle kiss
Would finally finally be lain upon
Your lips